THE NAME WE NEVER LOSE

Also by Nathaniel Hutner

War: A Book of Poems

Heracleitus Under Water

☙

The poems collected here are not mere versification, nor do they hide their meaning behind surrealism or cubism or any of the other movements of the twentieth century that made meaning oblique in the construction of an artistic reality. Rather, they offer to the reader of the new millennium a fresh way of organizing language and discovering its import. No one should doubt that the talent displayed in this volume is a growing one that will make its audience happy to come back for more.

THE NAME WE NEVER LOSE

ଔ

Nathaniel Hutner

Burlington, Vermont

Some of the poems which appear in this volume first appeared in the following periodicals: *The Yale Review*: Revenge; *POETALK - Bay Area Poets' Coalition*: A Zen State, Lucretia Locuples, Leider, True Tooth; *Chrysanthemum*: Other; *Breakthrough*: Heracleitus Under Water. Several of the ensuing poems were previously published in *Heracleitus Under Water*.

Copyright © 2019 by Nathaniel Hutner

All rights reserved. No part of this publication may be reproduced, distributed, or transmitted in any form or by any means, including photocopying, recording, or other electronic or mechanical methods, without the prior written permission of the publisher, except in the case of brief quotations embodied in critical reviews and certain other noncommercial uses permitted by copyright law.

Onion River Press
191 Bank Street
Burlington, VT 05401

Names: Hutner, Nathaniel, author.
Title: The Name We Never Lose : Poems / by Nathaniel Hutner.
Description: Burlington, VT: Onion River Press, 2019.
Identifiers: LCCN 2019931793 | ISBN 9781949066173
Subjects: LCSH American poetry. | Poetry--21st century. | BISAC POETRY / American / General.
Classification: LCC PS3608.U862 N36 2019 | DDC 811.6--dc23

Designed by Jenny Lyons, Middlebury VT

Printed in the United States of America

for Barbara

CONTENTS

Trashed 1

Kill Me Now 2

What My Love Will Send to Me 3

Underground 4

Kiss, Kiss 5

December 7

The Archbishop in Spite of Himself 8

And for Dessert… 9

The Name We Never Lose 10

Hippocrates 13

Dibble-dabble 14

Summertime 15

Trouble 16

Pearls 17

Trying to Hide? 18

Twins 19

Apple Trip 21

Other 23

Primus Inter Pares 24

Sixdenier	25
A Plangent Tear	28
Naked for a Day	29
Vertical Alert	30
Ode to Water	31
Self Delivery	33
Alabama in Painting	34
Opuscular Thoughts	36
Feline Maintenance	37
Color Role	38
A Short Translation	39
Doubt	40
Working Out Parallels	41
Naked	44
Obligato	45
The Blithedale Romance	46
Prolixin	47
A Hard Rap	48
My Nocturnal Migrations	50
The Mirror and the Mask	52

I tie my ear…	53
Blue Leaf	54
Antigone	56
A Long Key	57
True Tooth	58
Time to Beguine	59
The night becomes my soul…	60
Sculpt Me	61
I would like to feel…	62
Orpheus	63
Heracleitus Under Water	64
A Million Spots	65
The Musical Air	67
The Sea-Dragon	68
Buying Nothing	69
A Zen State	70
Lucretia Locuples	71
Leider	72
Revenge	73
Love	74

"...as we die in you,
You die in Time, Time in Eternity."

— LORD HERBERT OF CHERBURY,
To His Watch When He Could Not Sleep

THE NAME WE NEVER LOSE

Trashed

Hello, Daddy,
Are you surviving nicely?
Do you fill the black vacuum
Of my inner rage,
Perfecting the contest
Between age and age?
You leave tracks
I cannot follow,
O my little God.
I act and you direct:
I want to play myself
Before I'm dead.
My life is
Your property
Until one of us dies.
It makes no difference
Whether it's you or I.
Why, Daddy, you don't even love me: why?

Kill Me Now

When people try to give me tests
They always fail.
I don't know why; they are shortening
Their lives unduly.
It's like baking a soufflé
That falls.
The sky falls and the rain falls,
And none of us will see his soufflé again.

I wish I were not alone with the rain.
It is easier to laugh with someone.
A guide, perhaps, smelling of
French cherries and cinnamon.
Or a baker, who feeds
His pastries to the geese.

Will you be my guide?
Beyond the rain and the geese,
The cherries and webbed feet?
Will you kiss me?

Or kill me now
Before I lie,
Before I have to falsify
Who I am and how I've died
A thousand times beneath your eye.

What My Love Will Send to Me

First, he will send me his eyes,
So that I may see him in the dark;
Next he will send me his mouth,
So that I may speak with him in tongues;
Third, he will send me his lips,
So that I may kiss him;
Fourth, he will send me his ears,
So that I may hear the world moan
As we roll together;
Fifth, he will send me his hair,
So that I may touch something fine;
Then he will send me his soul,
So that I may know him whole;
Seventh, he will send me his heart,
So that we cannot be apart:
Time will send us the rest,
By which he and I will be blest.

Underground

Slight and sly,
The worm slips
Beyond my eye:
I try to find his hole
And come up with a mole.
Like the worm,
The mole lives beneath the surface
Of the wave,
He hides outside the scope of everyday,
Unless you think
The quotidian exists
A foot below
The grass and leaves
That other creatures
Find adequate for summer ease.

Kiss, Kiss

Fight for love?
Not me.
I'm perfectly pain-averse.
Your concern hurts.
I can see you coming.
I'm into singularity.
It's my own home.
I am about to turn blue—forever.
Then you will remain
Completely imaginary,
Like a crack in the dark.

December

December, month of ice,
Black cold, black device,
Tell me why you lie upon my eyes
So quietly. I think
You sleep peacefully,
Preparing me—
Am I to live again,
And rise from the ice and snow
And smell once more
The hyacinth,
The honeysuckle and the rose?
December, do not toy
With me. Leave me in peace
If life cannot come twice.
I think, in any case,
I would sooner die once
for all,
Than turn more than once
to ice.

The Archbishop in Spite of Himself

A tone down the corridor
Echoes the eye, the sense of what we see

Lies on the mind, pale next to the sun,
A shade. The heliotrope blooms,

And we turn to the red and say,
'How easy it is to be red'.

The red is what we have made,
And the heliotrope, as we saw it,

Was made, was made red,
And so on. This is when

We are this side of night;
At night the heliotrope turns blue,

The stars are white, and the sky
An even distance from the eye.

That, too, is what we make it,
Though what we make ourselves

Is ambiguous: out of our
Imagination, we imagine ourselves

As a metaphor for what we sense:
Warmth in the wind and air the color of absinthe.

And for Dessert…

Some people want the bomb,
but are perplexed because
they cannot find it anywhere.

Look under your chair, warrior,
you are missing a leg or two,
and if you get that damn bomb,
there will be no more of you.

The Name We Never Lose

I send my soul out
To be cleaned.
It does not mean anything
Before I wash
It in brine
And look to sand
To rub out all imperfections
Of being that I usually
Don't detect. I am tired
Of looking within.
I have exhausted
The spring with planting;
Now I must scrape
What I can from the seams
Of the earth that lie
Beneath my feet, hardened
By summer heat
And my own dead weight.
I am not free
To go away from myself.
Place me where you like,
Inside the dark or not,
It is no use:

I see the frame of the world
From where I stand,
And I await its interesting fate —
Fortune is too late
To blink. My enemies
Die intestate
And I seize their remains.
Love of God
Got them release beneath the earth
They walked on.
Their bare bodies bristle
As I pass over them.
One day I shall be buried
In the moon or in a place
Further away where I
Have not been
For a long time.
I was once young there,
And stayed
For a while.
Now that I have a decided
Age, I have learned
To live apart,
And dispose honestly
Of my war's dubious spoil.

All goods flow about me now,
I am liberated into the arms
Of friends, new memories
And a long past.
Expectation has grown
Into fact, and love ceases
To take its toll of me.
I tip forward,
And find I can move
Obstacles inside me that once
Were enough to keep me still.
Turn me once, you love-sick
Of history.
Life is like the sea —
Everything empties into it,
And nothing leaves,
— Except the pure mist.
We think we have won the war,
But we only lose
What we never know. And
What has come,
Has already gone before.

Hippocrates

I will write one more,
To make it five.
The same as
My maximum daily number
Of orgasms.
Imagination is not cheap,
And orgasm is dear.
And crudity in poetry
Has its precedents.
Even truth can obtrude
In the strangest places.
I think I am unwanted
Here or there.
Remember Hippocrates:
Do no harm,
And the patient may survive.
I shall write one more,
To make it five.

Dibble-dabble

Dibble-dabble,
Dibble-dabble,
It's me you meet
Upon your plate,
It's me you eat
Without compunction
Or regret.
Someday,
Our positions will reverse,
And then reverse again,
And we will spend eternity
Eating each other without end.

Summertime

Dry ice on a wet lawn—
    Freezing grass in the rain
Makes it hard to provide the mice
    With a haircut.
The moles are subaqueus
    And escape the cold,
And the worms are pink,
And the crickets leap in the leaves
And make love in the evening
    Underneath the windows
Where everyone can hear them—
    I wish I were a cricket
In the summertime,
    But then I would not live long.
Such are the penalties of copulation.

Trouble

I am waiting:
Give me tongue,
And you shall hear
The revolution
Of the spheres:
The word has neighbors
Everywhere,
In the atmosphere
And out—
I know the trouble
You're about.

Pearls

Pearls lie deep
Beneath the gray-back swell,
Or fall like tears
Into a weeping well,
Evanescent as the breath
Of the moon's white sphere,
They light the ocean's crest
Like moonbeams
Dressed in air.

Trying to Hide?

Trying to hide?
In my lap?

That's a red venue
For Puritans.

You can stay there
As long as you

Don't shake.
I do not solicit

Vibrations.

Twins

      i.

In the corner of my room,
Sits my eye.
It recognizes me in the evening
When the light dies.
It is not connected to anything.

      ii.

What a pain knowledge is.
It is as though someone
Had let the devil out
To watch us
And we had to cause trouble
So he would have a purpose.

      iii.

My other eye sees this,
But says nothing.
It is afraid of annihilation,
Which is going to come anyway,
So why not be brave
And face it?
Face it down,

And one day
We will have both our eyes back
Working for us
Facing down death,
Like the good eyes they are.

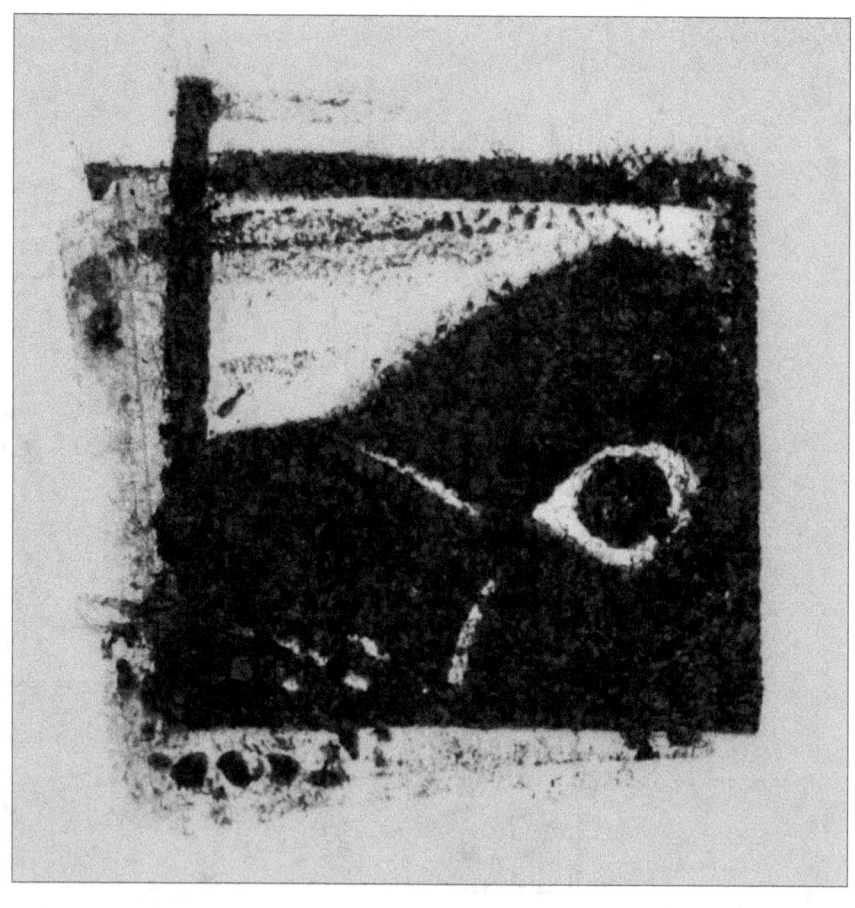

Apple Trip

What do we see in Apple?
The glorification of tree?
A seed for future use?
Present delicacy?

We have no tongue,
And our teeth are masticating
A past with no name:
What an appetite to tame!

We have left our friends behind.
They were not friends anyway.
Silence told us so.
Silence is a sign
My friends cannot read.
They just give it to me—
The usual human development.

"I built a temple all of gold
That none did dare to enter in."

It is light inside,
Even for those without glasses.

I try to speak so carefully!
And I give you a headache:
Try death. It is without headaches.
It is your commencement.
You take your degree
And move into a good neighborhood.

Do you still have time to kill?
Are you wading on the beach
By the murmuring sea?
Can you float onomatopoetically?
You are like a new bond
Or some other security.
Or are you counterfeit?

I know you are in the funds.
Your pain is in the wings.
Try them, and you will see
Farther into the heart of me
Than my own perfectibility.

Other

You will use my madness
To give me pain — you,
Who speak in the guise of truth
And wish me ill.
Have I not pain enough
For ten of you, or twenty?
Can you really be invulnerable?

You have given me the gift of my faults.
I have already lived with them,
They know me,
And I have made them my friends.
It is as if I lived with them
On a small island and we passed
Our time shifting places.

I am now all that I have been
And shall be,
History and potentiality.
My faults cannot destroy me.
Nor my madness.
Nor you.

Primus Inter Pares

    First Grade:

I'll never forget the four flights up
    my first day,
And the tall blond Amazon winging down
    eight flights my way,
Forcing me to choose
    right or left, I could not say.
I stood still, wondering if
    I could obey:

Then I smiled and shyly realized
    That I was free,
Since I could choose my Amazon,
    And my Amazon, me.

Sixdenier

Within the cloister they whisper
under their breaths to themselves
in gray robes
and hoods of scarlet or gold
and braids on the waist
worn for show;
They declaim in the garden
too far away to be heard,
Their hands rise and fall
silently in the light
after Vespers as night falls.

I see Cerberus at their door
three paces behind the last
from the sacristy
looking up at the crucifix
with a sigh--
Sign of what?
Let him bear it alone.

Now it's time for a crack to the right,
Let the taper shine there,
Then you have your answer:
> Three dice for a dime
> a nickel apiece
Cut them out and cast them
one by one

by the stench of the dead pig's belly
you'll see nothing but blind sailors
pilgrims and whores
all undone
from top
to bottom

twice he spoke
but no tongue
I'll play with his eyes,
the wandering Jew

The merry Widow's on her way back
To the secular wardrobe-room
to pick up a new exterior
incomparably superior to the old
What's she now?

A bundle of nerves
Strings from ear to ear
Yellow damask in the rear
makes a pretty sight of her
well-worn dilatory personnage
lateral green
longitudinal red
decked for a fool
born to dread
the fire in winter
in the summer the fog
hides her behind
its pearl of a guise
and makes her a sailor
in the dark on leave

A Plangent Tear

You ask me
To write a line.
From it fly
Pink sighs, blue tears
And yellow apostrophes.
A great freeze
Is hanging in the air:
Three weeks
Defined by a dry tear.

It fits, this sound.
I smell my enemies dying.
We love each other more now.

Naked for a Day

Time to dine? Nonsense.
I am not proper.
I have fallen out
With ambiguity.
Here I am,
Naked for a day,
Lolling without appetite.
Blood is hasty,
But my knife is empty.
Can your tongue be far behind?

Vertical Alert

    i.

An eye's body alive.
That's what arms us.
Then we are ready
For the piccolo,
For the final note
Before combat.

    ii.

Where are we at?
Honey, you tell me.
I'm jes climbin'
Them stairs
To eternity,
An' there ain't
No one gonna
Knock me off,
Even the stairs the'selves,
Jus' 'cause they's tricky.
On'y God gets all the way up.
An' he's stuck;
So I say,
Heave him ova
The hump
An' we'll all get home.

Ode to Water

Wherefore worry?
I am indulgent
Blue spruce, my love,
We are in the same basket.

This white planet
Is my subject,
But I am not its lord.
We are mutual communicants,
And dry and therefore white.

Where did we find ourselves out?
In the bath—quite a lie.
There are three things to remember from this:
(1) Don't forget to breathe;
(2) Remain still but vulnerable;
(3) Accept the love you can return.

Love is a pin that pricks.
And so on.
If you have a chair, don't use it for kindling:
Sit on it.
Even I freeze. It is best to be
Seasonally adjusted.

Keynes would have loved you,
His pitch is so sincere,
His mind mundane,
We observe him in parts,
Seeing what we wish to see.

The red moon is mounted
On a Keynesian base—
It has its cycles.
It pedals along,
Filling in the troughs
And mounting hills—
Why not be creative?

Well, water, come, I shall ask you:
How can I hide?
Where is the W.C.?

Self Delivery

Abuse my nerves!
They will fall on you.
I am an intricate web
Of consistency.
Flies catch me,
And I eat them up.
Down is another direction.
You will see this
When you falsify yourself for the
Last time.
Even armor-plate won't
Help you—it will lock you
Inside your problem.
You need care
Of every description.
What can you do?
What do you do?
Whatever it is,
Live on it.
It will deliver you.

Alabama in Painting

Entirely too blue, you see, she said,
Other colors count too,
Some even expand with their meanings
If you breathe them quickly.
Monster hopes are quick to reduce
With a sigh from white—
That is clean—and then we
Feel not what we imagine,
But what is there.

Yellow is the illumination of the
Universe, and travels around without
Apparent locomotion—it is
A queen, born to lead,
And it does so sweetly,
And discretely, even in
Shadow time.

Amber is yellow's cousin, and
Draws us into the shade.
That is the ease we need.

Brown is clean, also, though
It is the dirt's color.
But look who lives in the dirt!
Snakes and salamanders
And maiden-hair ferns,
Lichens and soldier moss,
All live in the shade.

Black is the negative number.
Is it death?
No, it is nothing, which anything
Can become.
Red is love, which anything
Can become.

We are beginning to understand
Those. Let us fix our understanding
Gently.
Are you arranged for green?
Yes, it is youth and anything new.
It requires useful instruction
Dutiful patience and care.
It is not without work,
But you will find in the end
That it will repay you all your love.

Opuscular Thoughts

Opuscular thoughts through
Oracular words work
Miraculous deeds with
The dead.

The live are the dead,
They lack heart, soul of head,
They have only a corpse,
(We have only remorse),
And they pour all their tears
Into infinite years
Of dear penury.

Feline Maintenance

My cat understudies
A dragon in disguise,
So don't cross his tracks
Or he'll kill you with his eyes.

Color Role

Blue will teach you
What is sin,
Red alludes to what's within,
Green is youth
And black the dark,
Brown the home of horny bark.
If you wish to know still more,
You must knock on love's back door.
Open it and look within,
There you'll see your crimson skin,
Luring men to strange demise,
Beyond the practice of their eyes.

A Short Translation

This can go there, and that, too.
Tell me, do you weep at particles?
Greek verbs do it most often:
A little jog of syntax
Sets them off.
The professors don't understand.
But they translate anyway,
Like the moon across the sky,
Only the moon arrives.
And the professors?
They don't translate
Like you and I.

Doubt

Beauty is the beast we all long for.
Wealth hides wrinkles within the exterior,
A fold or two in fame will still attract
A youth willing to bed an artifact,

Put the outside in,
Do not give up;
What nature will not give,
Fantasy offers as reprieve.

Working Out Parallels

Someone I know is
Hero of the pick-up,
Has dirty ears that don't hear,
Eyes that wipe reality
Out of existence, see
Substantial debt stateside,
And international recklessness.

We may reach very far
Into the stratosphere,
But is that Heaven?
It used to be, seen from here,
Until we went through it.
Now we are condemned
To contemplate the Universe.

Is it Heaven?
Somewhere we lost our future.
The truth can be highly beguiling,
Until it changes.
I am willing to change you,
If you are willing, too.
Life moves, and sometimes we are
Sitting on top of it.

Naked

It is probably the time
That makes me cry,
It is like love and
Needs no name.

Beyond apocalypse
Is the end we don't
Anticipate.

It is sweetness. I should
Look forward to this.
My mind runs backward
To the beginning:
I am swimming
In dreams, an empty wind
Unveiling itself before the world
As audience, unashamed.

Obligato

I'll start verso obligato,
Racing horses in my mind,
I cannot climb beyond my reason,
Seasoning will not cure this poison,
I am drowning in smoke,
Pale fires outlive me
As if to testify to suicide.
Enrich my history as you like,
I am a take between
Two tables; I run along
Like a young child,
Heedless. I will never
Eat the pear on the pear-tree,
Or the apricot or the apple;
The ice is dry that holds you lifeless
By the phlox and marigold.

The Blithedale Romance

I might be good on him,
But I'm not exactly like him.
I hear whispers down the street,
It is my enemies come to get me,
But they will never arrive.
I am a willow invisible
To the damned; the drowned
Are suspect because they
Are no longer alive.
Where does it go from here?
The suit is over, or at least played,
And the whole head
Is hurting beyond endurance.
I cannot move my fingers.
My prick is dense as marble.
I am seeing double rainbows—
It is after the shower now
And yet I am still unfinished.
I know I am safe,
But that means nothing to me.
I want love, I want fame,
I want everything.
I want to die.

Prolixin

Parlay your tongue
Into a weapon of war.
Turn the stone over
And crawl underneath
To find the slug's hiding place
And your soul's
Own darkness.
We are treading on our toes
As lightly as ballerinas
In the summer dusk.
They arrive too late
At the front door.
Time is closed now.
And the way out through the mouth
Is gone. The delectable
Light is flying by
You without a greeting.
You have yet to choose your end.
Let me only depress your tongue
With my aid
And you will fall mute
Into the final crisis.

A Hard Rap

Will you tell
The Guest to depart?
Love is unwelcome
In Elktown
And sex is sold:
The people could all be born
Of little seeds
In the ground,
And grow up wolves.
How is the soul conceived?
Outside time.
Some of us die
Without one.
It is a long way to go
For nothing.

My Nocturnal Migrations

Your eyes are marble eyes,
They are fixed with grey striations
Moving across two small expanses.
I move, too,
From one eye to two,
Afraid of the penalty
Of abjuration.
I will keep my mouth closed
In the shape of a rose,
Growing along the path
I have chosen.
What will is there?
What courage?
I must learn to row
Beyond the limits of a good name.
What I think is private
Unless you hear me do it
And see the sense behind it.
I am sure you will expose me
If I drop my eyes.
I am paralyzed by good behavior.
Sooner or later I may surrender

To my enemies
And bring them down.
I sweep daily,
And hope for a future occupation.
I don't think I can face death
Demonized.

The Mirror and the Mask

Will you accept the blank difference
Between one and one, this and that

Two measurables? We make things to measure
So that we may know them, as

The blue tapestry at Verdun,
Or Grandmother's black coffee table,

A new measure imposing a revolution
On past ponderables,

Leaving Verdun at one with the present
Of history. Blank materialists will laugh with Lenin:

They know what they know
And turn things upside down.

Then we see as in a mirror what we were
And are. Only the mask is different.

I tie my ear to a balloon.
From above it hears
The music of a broom.
Someone is sweeping below the moon,
I think it is the mistress
Of a poet's doom.

Blue Leaf

Blue leaf leave me,
Blue metal on the lawn,
The long way down
Is new to me
Though not new at all.

White fire of dew
On leaves, white steel
Of dew, turn to ice
On fallen trees,
Turn to ice in fall.

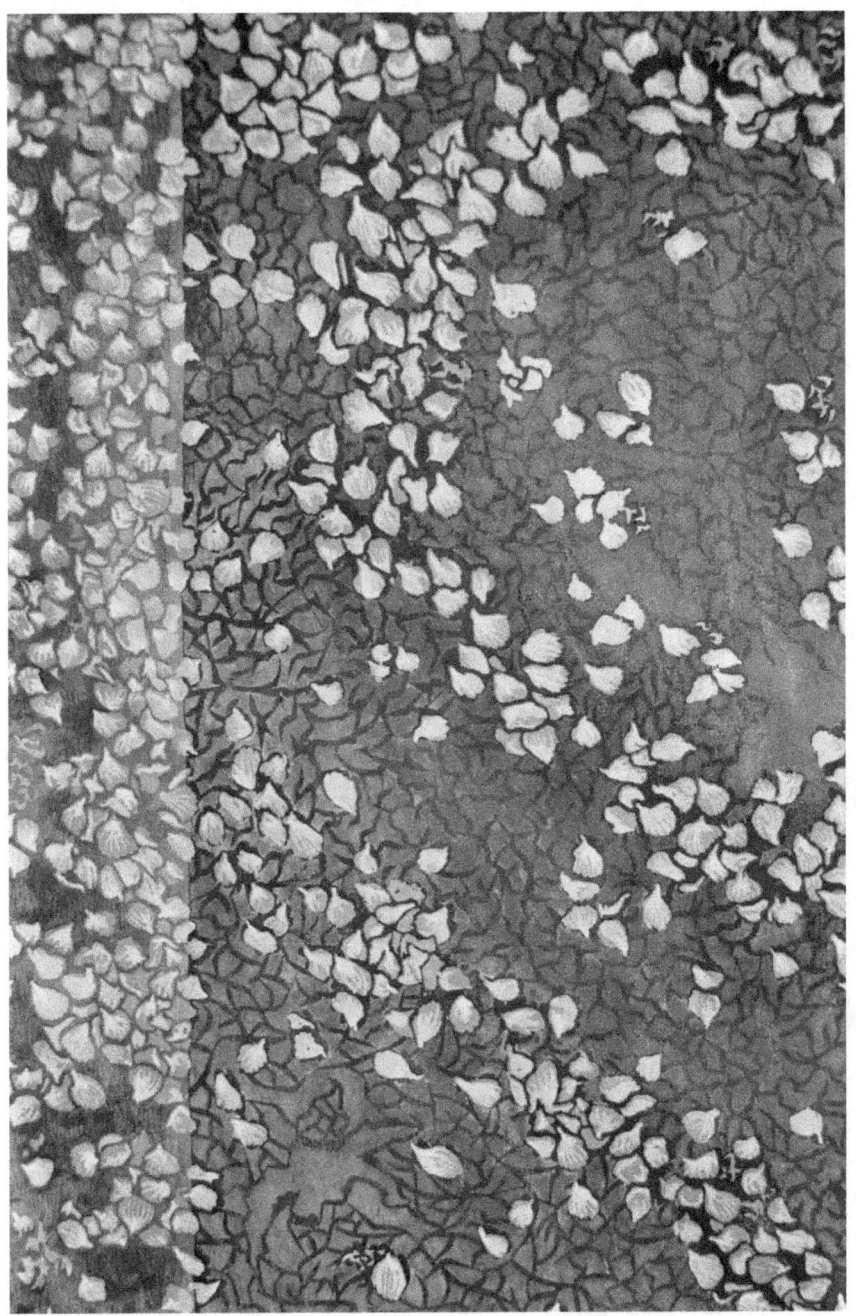

Antigone

Turn Antigone out.
Let her sleep
With the goat
And the sheep
In the folds
Of her soul
Which she holds
Over foul
Mortality.

Is she gone?
Not undone.

A Long Key

A poem exhibits different colors
At different angles. Each thought

Provokes its cousins variously, setting up
Dependencies like prophecies or memories.

True Tooth

Suppose, to start with,
A curve, of any nature,
Apple or plum,
Or what you think will do,
And then cut infinitely deep
Like a tooth:

Pit desire against itself
With care, light the fire,
And listen. What can we hear
In the flame? Its blue stands
For truth, not the blues,
And as we burn with the flame,
The blue becomes ever deeper
And transparent as Heaven.

Time to Beguine

Said Sweeney to Mrs. Porter,
"I shall swill your soda-water,
And then lie dead-drunk
In your lap,
My eye-lids open to your
Charms."

Mrs. Porter was having none of it.
"Tut," she said,
"You are, as far as the eye can see,
King of the Egyptians,
And I am your faithful adhaerens,
Stuck to you
Like glue
(What a mess!)"

"We shall have to do a bit piece,
A clean-up campaign,
With the field open
To all comers
And other prepotent people."

And so they did.

The night becomes my soul,
The day my empty whole,
To myself my ghost,
To others the most
Of what I am and am not.

Sculpt Me

Sculpt me, turn me on the wheel,
As the world spins, I begin to heal,
There is an art to how I feel,
Sculpt me, turn me, make me real.

I would like to feel completely well,
Like a young tamarisk tree,
Or a carillon of banging Russian bells.
Who will see my inside when I am out
Posturing in the dark?
Who will love me when I, too, am black at heart?
These are questions I have never dared to ask.
To whom can I vouchsafe my past?
There is not much in it for anyone:
A blind eye and exploded self.
I'll try to help
Myself as well as others. I promise not to hide
Behind reticences and the innocence of a child.
We all have much, I am sure, to bear,
As for me, I can say, 'I'm still here'.

Orpheus

Orpheus, lute on a string,
Eyes of a child,
Sits in the stream
Where lilies smile,
And skeets fly
Over green enameling,
White-pies and blue anemones,

And sings word-music,
Music to the world
Of dead souls,
Of black blood,
And the inimical chill that flows
From the yellow crusty shell
Of an unknown dead man's skull.

Heracleitus Under Water

Antiquities live off fat,
As the burnished breast will tell you,
Falling flaccid at the rise of age.
Three pebbles in a stream will tell you,
Burnished by the wave, how to hold out
Until the end, living under water,
Round with age.

So we see the polished chronometer
Of the stream's bed, lying under the lithe body
Of the water, into which we step
Again and again,
But never into the same.

A Million Spots

The artist slides,
And speckles, too,
A spot along
A million—two.

Inspection
Of my head I see
And wonder
What is wrong with me:

There's nothing new
That I can see,
I watch you, too,
As you watch me.

The Musical Air

The musical air turns wisdom to wit,
Draws laughter down to earth
And sanctifies it;
Humor is purified by way of pain,
Sun makes the poppy grow—
And so does the rain.

The Sea-Dragon

I am waiting, patient.
I am going to fish.
I am going to find
A sea-dragon on my line.
He will have eyes like knives,
A mouth greater than grief,
And each of his many scales
Bright as a viper's teeth.

It would please me if, without being dined upon,
I could love this fish as it would wish.

Buying Nothing

The dime will buy you nothing,
Except two nickels or ten pennies,
A small range of change
Available to any beggar in the street,
If he accepts dimes;
And if he does,
Is it strange
Should he reject the possibility of
Change?

A Zen State

I write by looking away
From the mark.
I move by indirection.
The eye leads away from
What is seen,
From imperfect to perfect
      imperfection.

Odd,
That what I see
I haven't got,
And what I have
I cannot see:
There is more than simple perplexity
In this for me.

Lucretia Locuples

Writing is another country,
A country without a name:
A lily is its outer face,
Its inner face a flame.

Leider

Our Nemesis is
an apple dumpling
in the fog—
A large decision
coming around
the corner.

Revenge

I am not supposed to be writing poetry,
I am supposed to be turning up my nose
And taking revenge.

But where my nose is going
There is no air,
And revenge is not possible.
There is enough revenge already.

I wish it were spring again,
And even that the rain would come
And clean us up.
I need a wash.
I think a lot, and a wash
Would make me feel better.

I can hear mice
Coming out of the woodwork.
They live there in winter
And come out at night
Looking for food.
The cat eats them.
I suppose it is instinct.
I suppose there is a lot of instinct everywhere,
But that is no excuse.

Love

Will they evaporate?
They may.
That is the lovely
End of white stars:
A blue heaven.
I wish I were a white star
Flying within my red heart,
My red heart within my blue heaven.

www.ingramcontent.com/pod-product-compliance
Lightning Source LLC
Chambersburg PA
CBHW052203110526
44591CB00012B/2063